Tomlinson and the

Framework for

Achievement

promoting adult learning

©2006 National Institute of Adult Continuing Education
(England and Wales)

21 De Montfort Street
Leicester
LE1 7GE

Company registration no. 2603322
Charity registration no. 1002775

NIACE has a broad remit to promote lifelong learning
opportunities for adults. NIACE works to develop increased
participation in education and training, particularly for those who
do not have easy access because of class, gender, age, race,
language and culture, learning difficulties or disabilities, or
insufficient financial resources.

You can find NIACE online at www.niace.org.uk

Cataloguing in Publication Data
A CIP record of this title is available from the British Library

Designed and typeset by Avon DataSet Ltd, Bidford-on-Avon, B50 4JH
Printed and bound in the UK by Cromwell Press, Trowbridge

ISBN: 1 86201 281 4

Tomlinson and the Framework for Achievement:

A unified answer to a divided system

Ann Hodgson, Ken Spours
and Peter Wilson

niace
promoting adult learning

Contents

Introduction: unified approaches in a divided context

This paper was conceived at a time when it was assumed that both the proposals from the Tomlinson Report on *14–19 Curriculum and Qualifications Reform,* primarily for young people, and the Framework for Achievement (FfA), primarily for adults, would be the main guiding policy frameworks for 14+ reform. Together, they were seen to provide two sets of curriculum and qualifications tools with which to build a more unified and seamless system to support lifelong learning. At that point, back in 2004, the most important question appeared to be the inter-relationship between these two reform agendas. This focus remains the guiding question for this paper because, despite setbacks for the Tomlinson reform agenda, we believe that these two related approaches to curriculum and qualifications reform can provide the basis for a more unified current and future 14+ agenda. The main purpose of this paper is to show where these two different unifying reform approaches came from, their different emphases, what they can jointly offer and how they can be brought together to serve the needs of all learners from 14+.

Although the White Paper *14–19 Learning and Skills* (DfES, 2005a) has signalled the Government's intention to retain a divided curriculum and qualifications system for younger learners, the adult agenda is less constrained. The FfA, introduced as part of the Skills White Paper, *21st Century Skills* (DfES, 2003a), potentially offers a way of keeping the unified tradition alive through the creative use of credit in the design of specialised diplomas. We argue that the application of key features of the FfA can produce an openness in the design of diplomas which allows not only a broader approach to vocational education and training, but also the eventual integration of general education, including GCSEs and A Levels.

In Section One of this paper, we describe the historical roots of both unified traditions. We do this in some detail because we feel it is important for those involved in reform to exercise 'policy memory' (Higham and Yeomans, 2005) and to build on and learn from past experiences. Section Two examines the recent history of 14–19 qualifications reform, culminating in the publication of the Tomlinson Final Report in 2004. In this section we also reflect on the use of the different 'languages' associated with diplomas and credit in the Tomlinson reform process. Section Three focuses on the emergence of credit as a tool for reform. Section Four describes how some of the key features of the FfA can be applied to the new 14–19 White Paper specialised diplomas in such a way that these new qualifications take on Tomlinson-like features. We conclude by suggesting that if the features of the FfA are fully applied to the specialised diplomas, the integration of general qualifications looks historically inevitable. Thus, the coming together of the two unified reform traditions will not only help to overcome the academic/vocational divide, but will also produce the conditions for the further development of an inclusive lifelong learning system.

The English unified reform tradition

The roots of the recent Tomlinson 14–19 curriculum and qualifications reforms lie in the English unification debates of the late 1980s and 1990s, which revolved primarily around responses to academic/vocational divisions and concerns about raising levels of post-16 participation, achievement and progression to match those of other European countries. These debates, while very much based on the history and needs of the national education and training system, can also be seen as part of wider European discussions about how to reform upper secondary education in the context of global socio-economic and technological changes (Lasonen, 1998).

In this part of the paper we trace the development of what we term an 'English unified reform tradition' from the late 1980s through to the Tomlinson proposals for a unified diploma system in 2004. By the English unified reform tradition we refer to the debates about, and proposals for, 14+ curriculum and qualifications reform which, we argue, has two major strands – a 'baccalaureate/grouped award' approach mainly associated with younger learners and a 'unitised/open framework' approach mainly associated with older learners. In this section we focus primarily on the evolution of the baccalaureate/grouped award approach but also comment on the important contribution of the unitised/open framework approach.

This historical account suggests that the Tomlinson proposals for an inclusive, flexible but coherent 14–19 diploma system are the latest phase of development within the English unified reform tradition drawing upon six major influences:

- the Technical and Vocational Initiative (TVEI) with its stress on common learning processes across 14–19 academic and vocational programmes;
- *A British Baccalaureate* (Finegold *et al.*, 1990) which provided a blueprint of a unified diploma system for the English context;
- proposals for a credit framework which introduced the concept of ascribing credit value to units of assessment (FEU, 1992);
- a 'core' and 'specialisation' diploma model designed as part of the *Learning for the Future Project* (Richardson *et al.*, 1995);
- the concept of a two-stage reform approach highlighted in Labour's pre-election policy document, *Aiming Higher* (Labour Party, 1996);
- the International Baccalaureate with its core that includes an extended essay.

Arguably, there was also a seventh influence on the Tomlinson designs for a unified diploma system – an analysis of the strengths and weaknesses of the *Curriculum 2000* reform process and the desire to learn from past mistakes (Hodgson and Spours, 2003).

The public debate about a unified baccalaureate/grouped award approach to 16–19 education and training in England started in earnest with *A British Baccalaureate* published by IPPR in 1990. This landmark document was a response to the problems of what was termed the 'academic/vocational divide' which referred to the sharp divisions between academic and vocational qualifications in the UK, notably A Levels and NVQs. *A British Baccalaureate* argued that this divide led to low levels of participation and achievement in education and training in comparison with other countries, impoverished academic programmes, low-status vocational education and inequality and inefficiency of outcomes from post-compulsory education and training (Finegold *et al.*, 1990). The solution was the creation of a unified curriculum and qualifications system to reform academic and vocational learning simultaneously.

Common curriculum processes: late 1980s

The 1980s, which formed the backdrop for *A British Baccalaureate*, were not only a period of division but also of innovative curriculum developments. The Technical and Vocational Education Initiative (TVEI) and the Certificate of Pre-Vocational Education (CPVE) attempted to introduce common curricular experiences for learners on both academic and vocational programmes (e.g. the concept of an 'entitlement curriculum' comprising recording of achievement, work experience, core skills and ICT) together with experiential and practical forms of learning (Crombie-White *et al.*, 1995). This period also saw the emergence of experimental BTEC diploma models, which combined modular flexibility with the concept of coherent learner programmes (Burgess, 1993). Practitioner involvement in and promotion of these innovations contributed to a professional consensus for the reform of the 14–19 phase based upon a 'bottom-up' concept of a process-based entitlement curriculum together with a national unified qualifications model that confronted the academic/vocational divide (Howieson *et al.*, 1997).

In the wake of the Conservative Government's rejection of the Higginson reform of A Levels (DES, 1988) and the introduction of a more formalised national divided triple-track qualifications system in the early 1990s (DfE/ED/WO, 1991) – comprising A Levels, GNVQs and NVQs – it was clear that a unified approach to 14–19 education was off the political agenda and bottom-up reform became much more difficult (Hodgson and Spours, 1997). As we will see, this historical reflection bears an uncanny resemblance to the reform process of 2005.

Unified qualifications and unitisation blueprints: early to mid 1990s

The response from the reformers was a wave of radical proposals and blueprints for a unified curriculum and qualifications system, starting with *A British Baccalaureate* but swiftly followed by others (e.g. Royal Society, 1991; FEU, 1993; AfC *et al.*, 1994; NAHT, 1995; NCE, 1995; NUT, 1995; Jenkins and David, 1996; JACG, 1997). These proposals for reform can broadly be divided into two types – a more 'grouped/prescriptive' or a more 'open/framework' approach. Those who argued for the former wanted learners to take a combination of subjects in the 14–19 phase to

5

ensure breadth of study and to address the culture of dropping 'difficult' subjects such as mathematics, sciences and modern foreign languages. This approach can be seen in *A British Baccalaureate* and in proposals from the Royal Society, National Commission on Education, the National Association of Headteachers, the *Welsh Baccalaureate* proposals from Jenkins and David, and in the Dearing Report (1996). On the other hand, those who argued for an open/framework approach were in favour of a unified, flexible and unitised model which promoted the elective, open and choice-based features of the English qualifications system (e.g. FEU, 1992, 1993; AfC *et al.*, 1994; JACG, 1997).

Integrating unification reform approaches: 1995–1997

In the mid-1990s, as part of the *Learning for the Future* project, attempts were made to design a 'compromise' diploma model based on a core/specialisation design that integrated aspects of both unification reform approaches. It also aimed to supersede the domain-based design of *A British Baccalaureate*, which, in retrospect, can be seen to be primarily concerned with broadening general education. The core/specialisation model was flexible enough to encompass all aspects of vocational and occupationally specific learning, whilst still retaining a core of common general education (Young and Spours, 1996). In addition, representatives of both the 'unifiers' and the 'frameworkers' came together in 1996/97 during the debate surrounding the Dearing Review of 16–19 qualifications to agree on a set of principles for reform of education and training for 14–19 year olds. As a result, a joint statement from the main education professional associations, brokered by the Institute of Education, University of London, was produced in 1997 (AoC *et al.*, 1997). It suggested that a curriculum and qualifications framework for England should:

- commence at 14 rather than 16, as learners begin to specialise in their studies;

- act as a framework for 'a curriculum entitlement' in what was an elective and fragmented education and training system;
- reduce the division between academic (now termed 'general') and vocational learning so that all learners could develop both theoretical and applied capacities and also to promote parity of esteem for vocational education and training;
- be represented by a single and easily recognisable form of certification (e.g. a baccalaureate or diploma) which embraced both full-time and part-time learning and general and vocational achievement;
- be multi-level and non-age-related in order to build a ladder of achievement for all learners;
- be modular in order to support breadth, depth and more flexible approaches to study.

These fundamental principles of curriculum and qualifications reform in England have, as we will see, proved to be enduring and underpinned much of the critique of both *Curriculum 2000* and the recent Green Paper *14–19: Extending Opportunities, Raising Standards* (DfES, 2002a) and then went on to inform the Tomlinson Working Group on 14–19 Reform.

During the 1990s there were, however, limits to both the scope and depth of the professional consensus for curriculum and qualifications reform from 14+. Most of the proposals were 'blueprints' and did not go into a great deal of design or operational detail. The only exception was the proposals for *A Welsh Baccalaureate* (Jenkins and David, 1996), derived from the International Baccalaureate approach. Moreover, amidst the consensus on basic principles, there were important unresolved issues that were relatively neglected. The debates and designs focused mainly on advanced level and full-time general education, despite an appreciation in principle that a unified 14+ curriculum and qualifications framework should span different levels and embrace both full-time education and the work-based route. Little attention was devoted to the lower levels and the curriculum for 14–16 year olds, and discussions about an approach to certificating apprenticeship remained unexplored except one attempt by a group of academics to write *A British Baccalaureate* for the work-based route (Evans *et al.*, 1997). Moreover, this lack of detail and scope meant that there was also relatively little discussion of the reform process itself, the architecture of the system or implementation issues. All these deficiencies had to be addressed by the Tomlinson Working Group.

New Labour and the unified reform tradition: 1997–2003

In the period prior to the 1997 General Election, the Labour Party, in its policy document *Aiming Higher,* adopted an approach to 14–19 education reform which drew upon this professional consensus (Labour Party, 1996). *Aiming Higher* argued for a two-stage strategy, spanning two Parliaments, to move from the existing divided curriculum and qualifications system, through a framework stage, to a unified diploma system. New Labour's Election Manifesto, however, reduced this relatively ambitious 14–19 approach to the more limited aims of *'broadening A Levels; up-grading vocational qualifications and introducing key skills within a rigorous framework'* (Labour Party, 1997).

This approach to curriculum and qualifications reform was closer to the Dearing reform agenda for 16–19 advanced level qualifications than to the *Aiming Higher* vision of a 14–19 diploma system (Hodgson and Spours, 1999). The *Qualifying for Success* (DfEE, 1997) consultation and reforms, which became Labour Party policy in this area and eventually became known as *Curriculum 2000,* brought about a suspension of the debates on 14+ baccalaureates/frameworks as the new government restricted its reforms to advanced level and to individual qualifications. Overarching certification proposals were effectively put on the back burner for a second Parliament (Blackstone, 1998). The debate was also restricted by the profession itself as discussion moved from principles of a unified curriculum and qualifications framework and focused instead on implementation of the new advanced level qualifications, comprising the new A Level made up of AS/A2 blocks, the Advanced Certificate of Vocational Education (AVCE), the Key Skills Qualification and the Advanced Extension Award (AEA) (Hodgson and Spours, 2003). In private, the reformers were reassured by Ministers and advisers that *Curriculum 2000* was part of a step-by-step approach to more fundamental

14–19 curriculum and qualifications reform, but without the declaration of a clear end point.

While the late 1990s and early 2000s were dominated by the preparation for and implementation of *Curriculum 2000*, baccalaureates (or more precisely, overarching certificates) continued to be promoted in a piecemeal way. In 1999, the curriculum and qualifications regulatory authorities in England, Wales and Northern Ireland commissioned research on an overarching certificate (OAC) at advanced level but within a highly-constrained remit (QCA/ACCAC/CCEA, 1998). The resulting research report recommended a core/specialisation model containing a 'connective study', the latter of which owed much to the International Baccalaureate's extended essay (FEDA/IoE, 1999). In the same year, the Social Exclusion Unit in its report *Bridging the Gap* (SEU, 1999), recommended the development of a 'graduation certificate' to be aimed principally at marginalised 16–19 year olds. This proposal drew on some of the OAC design features and added dimensions concerned with extra-curricular activities which echoed the English TVEI 'recording of achievement' tradition of the late 1980s and early 1990s (Hodgson and Spours, 2000). Meanwhile, there were a number of other baccalaureate/diploma-related developments. These included the *Welsh Baccalaureate Award* (Adams, 2003); proposals for an Apprenticeship Diploma; and a variety of local bottom-up developments, an enduring feature of the English reform tradition, which continued to take place despite lack of clear support from national government (e.g. Stewart, 2003; Butler, 2003).

Summary

Throughout the period from the late 1980s to 2003, it is thus possible to trace the influence of two distinct broad, but related, strands of reform thinking on curriculum and qualifications reform: one based more on a baccalaureate or 'grouped award' approach with a focus on curriculum, coherent programmes of study and the needs of younger learners; the other emphasising an 'open', flexible and unitised framework aimed mainly at the needs of adult learners. Each of these reform traditions had its own priorities and language. The first prioritised curriculum, coherence and

9

quality of learning. Its language was predominantly one of 'inputs', because its prime purpose was to design and deliver breadth, depth and balance in programmes of study. The open, unitised framework tradition, on the other hand, prioritised learner access, progression and choice. Its language was one of 'outcomes', because its main purpose was to recognise different types of learning achieved in any context or by any mode, which is particularly important for adult learners.

The Tomlinson proposals for a 14–19 diploma system, as we shall see below, drew upon both of these traditions but prioritised the first because of the focus on younger learners and their educational formation. However, The Tomlinson Final Report (Working Group on 14–19 Reform 2004a) recognised that younger learners also need certain aspects of flexibility and choice that are to be found in the 'open' unitised tradition. Moreover, at the time when the Tomlinson Final Report was published, the unitisation of the National Qualifications Framework was part of official government policy (QCA and LSC, 2004) and the Government was seeking to relate both reform agendas *to achieve seamless progression from 14–19 learning into the adult framework'* (QCA, 2004, p.7). While government policy now appears less clear in this area, we would argue that these two approaches still need to be articulated in practice to facilitate lifelong learning. In the final part of this paper, we will demonstrate how the use of credit might be used to achieve Tomlinson-like principles and design features in the 14–19 White Paper context.

SECTION TWO

The Tomlinson reform proposals

In this section of the paper we discuss how the Tomlinson proposals for 14–19 curriculum and qualifications reform drew on both aspects of the English unified reform tradition in an attempt to improve both the quality and demand of the curriculum, together with a focus on inclusive learner participation, achievement and progression.

Here we take as our starting point the publication of the Green Paper *14–19: Extending Opportunities, Raising Standards* (DfES, 2002a) because this was the first official recognition by government of the need for a 14–19 phase of education. This consultation document, which was published in the Spring of 2002, effectively formalised the age of 14 as the end of the national curriculum, allowing schools to offer a wider range of courses and qualifications in Key Stage 4 and emphasising the importance of flexibility and individual choice to encourage more young people to stay on in education and training.

This first attempt by government to outline a strategy for 14–19 education and training had a mixed reception from the education profession. While proposals to diversify 14–16 education were welcomed, respondents were very critical of what they saw as 'weak' ideas for matriculation diplomas and an overall lack of a coherent curriculum vision for the 14–19 phase. Added to this was the 'crisis' of the A Level grading system in the summer and autumn of 2002 when thousands of examination papers had to be scrutinised because of accusations that the awarding bodies had deliberately lowered grades in some A Level subjects. This attack on the A Level 'Gold Standard', together with the appointment of David Miliband, a co-author of *A British Baccalaureate*, as Minister for School Standards, opened a window of opportunity for a more radical approach to 14–19 education policy.

The Government responded by publishing, *14–19, Opportunity and Excellence* (DfES, 2003), which proposed that the short-term choice and flexibility agenda outlined in its earlier Green Paper should be complemented by a longer-term strategy for more structural reform of the 14–19 curriculum and qualifications system. It proposed the formation of a working group to take forward this agenda under the leadership of Mike Tomlinson, a former Chief Inspector of Ofsted.

The Working Group on 14–19 Reform began its deliberations in the spring of 2003 with a remit to strengthen full-time vocational education and offer more coherence in learning programmes for all young people; to consider the assessment arrangements for 14–19 year olds and to make recommendations for a unified framework of qualifications. In order to be inclusive of different interests and to develop a workable consensus in the short period of time it had been given, the Working Group comprised 14 individuals from a range of backgrounds, together with a dedicated group of civil servants drawn from the DfES and QCA. The main Working Group was supported by three sub-groups, each focusing on a strand of the remit. In addition, a number of stakeholder groups (e.g. higher education, business, young people) were formed to give feedback on proposals as they emerged.

At much the same time, QCA, with the support of the Learning and Skills Council (LSC) and the Sector Skills Development Agency (SSDA), had been tasked to develop a *'new flexible, responsive and coherent framework for recognising qualifications and achievement for adults'* (QCA, 2004, p.1) arising from the challenges outlined in the Government's skills strategy *21st Century Skills: Realising our Potential* (DfES *et al.*, 2003). It was inevitable that these two government reform agendas would, at some time, have to be brought together or at least aligned to facilitate learner progression.

The 14–19 Working Group reports: diplomas and credit

In its first progress report, *Principles for Reform of 14–19 Learning Programmes and Qualifications,* published in July 2003, the Working

Group highlighted a number of key problems in 14–19 education and training, as well as setting out the broad principles for reform with the central concept of a multi-level framework of diplomas comprising components rather than free-standing qualifications. This first report acted as a formal consultation document to gauge support for the direction of reform. While there was no specific mention of credit in the progress report, there was a significant discussion of the importance of designing a curriculum and qualifications framework which balanced features of a 'climbing frame approach' and 'baccalaureate-type characteristics' in order to offer both flexibility and coherence.

The interim report, *14–19 Curriculum and Qualifications Reform*, published in February 2004, set out in some detail the basic design of a new diploma system spanning entry to advanced level and all types of learning for 14–19 year olds; a template for diploma programmes comprising Core and Main Learning and an assessment model which attempted to reduce the assessment burden of existing qualification arrangements. It is this document which first indicated the need for *'maintaining continuity between 14–19 and adult learning'* and recognised the importance of reconciling *'the unitisation and credit-based approaches proposed for adult learning'* with the *'emphasis on whole programmes and diplomas for young people'* (Working Group on 14–19 Reform, 2004a, p.29). At this point, however, no specific recommendations were made about the use of credit within the proposed 14–19 diploma system. Rather, the report referred to the issue of the interface with adult learning because of the parallel work being undertaken by QCA.

The final report, *14–19 Curriculum and Qualifications Reform*, published in October 2004, however, contained specific mention of credit as a tool for recognising achievement as well as a means of progression within and beyond the diploma system.

The Tomlinson reform proposals

Before discussing the use of credit within the proposed Tomlinson diploma system, it is important to describe in a little more detail the broad reform proposals contained in the final report. The point to be appreciated is the wide-ranging and ambitious nature of reform proposals as the Working Group attempted to respond both to its remit and to its analysis of the weaknesses of existing education and training arrangements. The final report can be seen to be pursuing no fewer than 13 major system improvements for the newly created 14–19 phase:

1. developing coherent and high quality learning programmes;
2. strengthening vocational education and providing more practical and work-related learning for all learners;
3. promoting learner inclusion, participation and achievement and tackling disengagement;
4. improving the quality and relevance of teaching and learning;
5. ensuring learner acquisition of basic skills and broader skills for progression;
6. increasing stretch and challenge for all learners;
7. improving assessment arrangements by reducing the assessment burden and stressing the importance of assessment for learning and the role of teacher professional judgement;
8. creating a system of more transparent and simplified accreditation outcomes;
9. securing clear progression routes for all learners;
10. providing increased learner personalisation, choice and flexibility;
11. meeting the needs of end-users such as employers and higher education providers;
12. articulating 14–19 education and training with employment, higher education and Key Stage 3;
13. developing a long-term and carefully managed reform process.

Some of these aims were deemed to require a more coherent approach to curriculum and qualifications for 14–19 year olds, while others were seen to demand a more flexible structure, reflecting a balance between the 'baccalaureate' and the 'climbing frame' approaches highlighted in the progress report. In attempting to take this course, in its interim report, the Working Group had already set out two extreme positions, which it sought to avoid, while making use of the best features of both.

On the one hand, the Working Group did not want '*a highly open credit framework in which large qualifications are constructed from the bottom up by accumulating smaller units or credits to reach a specified volume and level of learning needed to achieve a diploma'* on the grounds that it *'would offer only very weak guarantees about the content and nature of individual programmes'* (Working Group on 14–19 Reform, 2004a, p.25). On the other hand, it argued against *'a highly prescribed baccalaureate-style approach in which the content and structure of each diploma would be clearly delineated and separately designed as a full programme in its own right'* because this model *'would have little scope for personalisation or for transferring partial achievement from one diploma to another at the same level'*. What it argued for was the *'need to take elements from both to achieve an appropriate range of choice and flexible progression, on the one hand; and, on the other, a coherent and distinctive range of options for specialised learning underpinned by a common core'* (Working Group on 14–19 Reform, 2004a, p.25).

The final designs for the diploma system thus centred around four key architectural features:

First, the report proposed the creation of a unified, multi-level 14–19 diploma system spanning Entry to Advanced Level in which each level of the diploma interlocks with the one above to promote inclusion and progression.

Second, it also argued for the development of two types of diploma – open and specialised – that recognise both broad and specialist programmes of learning to provide choice and relevance in the 14–19 phase.

Third, the system of diplomas was based upon a Core/Main Learning template. This was described in terms of required components at different levels and minimum volumes of learning. Credit values were used to recognise achievement in learning programmes to be recorded on a diploma transcript. This was to allow movement both within and beyond the diploma system.

Fourth, the diploma system used an assessment model which attempted to reduce the incidence of external assessment throughout the 14–19 phase but particularly at the lower levels; promoted 'assessment for learning'; provided a stronger role for teacher judgement; used grading for both motivation and for selection; and introduced institutional validation as a major tool of quality assurance.

The 14–19 diploma system: the languages of curriculum and credit

In its Final Report, the Tomlinson Working Group drew on language and concepts from both aspects of the unified reform tradition to describe its proposals for a 14–19 diploma system.

It used a 'curriculum and qualifications language'-guided learning hours; Core and Main Learning; Open and Named diplomas; diploma components; rules of combination; minimum diploma requirements, some of which are assessed and some of which are not; and assessment and validation approaches. This language was primarily used to describe what learner programmes would look like, what would be needed to deliver and resource them and how they would be assessed and quality assured.

However, the Report also used the language of 'credit' to:

- describe the volume and level of learner achievement up to and beyond the diploma thresholds in a consistent and transparent manner;
- facilitate flexibility of study in different modes and contexts, including movement between institutions;
- support accumulation of learning and achievement over time;
- promote both vertical and horizontal progression within the diploma system itself;
- provide a common language in which learner achievements could be 'exported' from the diploma system into the adult framework or 'imported' from the adult framework into the diploma system.

One of the main mechanisms for joining the two languages together was the learner transcript in which learner achievement was described in terms of Core/Main Learning, components, grade, narrative and credit.

A number of observations can be made about the deliberations of the Working Group on diplomas and credit over the 18 months of its work. Throughout, it sought to balance and synthesise the two aspects of the unified reform tradition – one that prioritised learning coherence and the other that prioritised flexible movement – in order to meet its wide-ranging aims. Its early work on the basic design, content and purpose of the diploma system and template drew more upon the baccalaureate/grouped award tradition, albeit going with the grain of the English qualifications tradition of learner choice and specialisation. Major consideration was given to the concept of whole learner programmes, comprising specifically-designed components in order to ensure that younger learners had the opportunity to develop the knowledge, skills and attributes required for progression and adult life which could not be guaranteed under a system of individual qualifications. At the same time, the Working Group was concerned to reduce the burden of assessment and thought that a unitised system might conflict with these aims. Thus concepts of credit and unitisation remained implicit and relatively under-utilised and unexplored. The Working Group did not discuss if or how components would be broken down into units. It was only when thinking moved on to how learners would achieve within the diploma system, together with the challenge of articulation with adult learning, that the concepts of units and credit had to be actively considered.

On the surface, there appears to be a division of labour between the language of curriculum and qualifications and the language of unitisation and credit – one appears primarily concerned with 'inputs' and the other with 'outputs'. However, on closer scrutiny, the pragmatic approach of the Working Group to these key concepts resulted in a number of issues to be addressed or clarified. These included:

- how to deal with grading which is not part of a credit system but which is part of a curriculum and qualifications system for young people;
- how to resolve the issue of gradient of study within Level 3, represented currently by the AS/A2 arrangements in *Curriculum 2000* and the A1/A2 arrangements in the proposed Tomlinson advanced diplomas, which is at odds with the idea that credit is based upon a single level at each point in the national qualifications framework;
- how to reconcile the proposal that the component is the smallest recognised block of achievement within the diploma system with the fact that the unit is the smallest block within the FfA.

It is to these issues, together with those raised from the perspective of the FfA, that we turn our attention in the next section of this paper.

The role of credit in the process of reform

Having analysed the continuity of key aspects of the 'baccalaureate' strand of post-14 reform thinking in recent years, we now seek to show how this particular tradition relates to the development of a system of credit accumulation and transfer that is seen by government as the cornerstone for developing a new approach to the National Qualifications Framework (NQF). Before doing so, it is first necessary to identify some key points in the separate history of credit in recent years.

The insertion of the concept of credit into the current process of qualifications reform originates in July 2003 within the Skills Strategy White Paper *21st Century Skills: Realising our Potential* (DfES *et al.*, 2003). In Chapter Five of the White Paper, the Government sets out a programme for reform of 'the qualifications system' and includes within this an explicit commitment to the development of 'a credit framework for adults'. This is a significant moment, as it marks the first commitment of government in England to the development of credit as an integral part of the process of qualifications reform. However, it is also an ambiguous commitment, balancing as it does an overall concept of reform of 'our qualifications system' with an implicit recognition that part of this process of reform – qualifications for 14–19 year olds – is to be taken forward through a separate reform process, based on the March 2005 White Paper *14–19 Education and Skills* (DfES, 2005a).

Indeed, the Skills Strategy White Paper inserts the concept of credit into another existing process of reform. Following the Quinquennial Review of QCA (DfES, 2002b), the DfES established a remit for the further reform of vocational qualifications and of the occupational standards that underpin them. QCA and its partner regulators in Wales and Northern Ireland, however, were already moving tentatively towards some modest reforms of the NQF. To add to this already complex picture, the DfES made it clear in its remits to QCA and the Learning and Skills Council (LSC) that in taking forward the development of 'an adult credit framework' they expected the framework to encompass a range of achievements both inside and outside the current NQF.

By the end of 2003 there were, therefore, three separate strands of reform underway within the qualifications system – those for 14–19 year-olds, for vocational qualifications and for adults. These reforms were further complicated by remits that related to England only (for 14–19 year-olds and adults) to England, Wales and Northern Ireland (for the reform of vocational qualifications) and to the whole of the UK (for occupational standards). The potential for confusion in the reform process was significant.

During 2004, there was a concerted and explicit attempt to draw together these different strands of reform into a single coherent process. The first step was to try and merge the separate remits for reform of vocational qualifications and the development of an adult credit framework. The second step was to bring together the remits of QCA and LSC into a single process for the development of a credit framework. However, these revised remits still related to England only, with separate remits for reform in relation to credit being taken forward in Northern Ireland and (more significantly) in Wales. The White Papers on skills and 14–19 education and training confirmed that new specialised diplomas in England would be encompassed within the reform process. A Levels and GCSEs, however, were explicitly excluded. By the autumn of 2005, these separate reform agendas sat together more closely, though in some instances still uncomfortably, within the proposal to establish a new framework for achievement that would, in time, replace the existing NQF (QCA and LSC, 2004).

The importance of the concept of 'credit' to the reform process

At each stage of this reform process, the concept of 'an adult credit framework' contained within the July 2003 White Paper has remained constant. There is now a clear consensus that the reform of all vocational qualifications will be based on a system of credit accumulation and transfer (DfES, 2005b), and that credit will be a key feature of the process for drawing into a reformed NQF a range of achievements that currently fall outside its scope. There is also an opportunity to use credit within the new specialised diplomas announced in the 14–19 White Paper. However partial this process might be, it may create the basis for development of qualifications for 14–19 year olds within the specifications of the FfA. Despite the timidity of the 14–19 White Paper in taking forward the Tomlinson agenda, it does mark another formal advance in the development of credit in England. For the first time, government policy recognises the relevance of credit to 14–19 year-olds in full-time education and training.

In this policy context, we suggest that credit can play an important role in taking forward the unified reform agenda in England for a radical and comprehensive reform of qualifications within a genuinely inclusive national framework. The key test of the concept of credit in this context will be its ability to shape the 14–19 qualifications emerging from the 2005 White Paper. In order to understand how credit can be used to support this process of reform, it is necessary to identify some key moments in the recent history of credit systems in the UK and to establish the concept of credit as a tool of reform.

The idea of a national credit framework

We may trace the origins of credit systems in post-school education and training in the UK back to two sources. One of these was the development of the Credit Accumulation and Transfer System of the Council for National Academic Awards (CNAA) that drew heavily on the model of credit in North American universities and colleges (CNAA, 1989). The second source of development of credit systems can be located to a similar point in time, with the establishment of the first Open College Networks (OCNs) in the early 1980s (NIACE, 1991). Although these were very much local initiatives, with no central agency to support or structure developments, the current work on credit within the qualifications reform process still draws heavily on the OCN model.

By the late 1980s the growth of OCNs was beginning to accelerate and the National Open College Network (NOCN) was established (NIACE, 1991). It is interesting to note from the perspective of 2005 that, even after the formal establishing of NOCN, local OCNs still operated different types of credit system, and indeed some members of NOCN did not award credits at all. This gives us a clue to an important feature of this development – that the commitment of OCNs to social inclusion and widening participation for adult learners was at least as important to their development as the credit system with which they are now so closely identified.

At the beginning of the 1990s we find the first use of the term 'national credit framework' within the literature of OCNs (UDACE, 1991). A few months later the Further Education Unit published *A Basis for Credit?* (FEU, 1992) and there then followed several years of increasingly vocal demands from many organisations across the post-school sector for the formal establishment by government of a national credit framework (AfC *et al.*, 1994). In retrospect, we can now see the development of these demands as an alternative focus for reform to the 'official' process of developing first the NCVQ framework, then GNVQs, then the NQF itself, and most recently *Curriculum 2000*.

In establishing this alternative focus for reform, the credit system represented itself explicitly as a unifying concept. Within a credit framework all achievements in any curriculum area could be recognised. Although OCNs represented their offer of accreditation at lower levels of achievement (in part to prevent any accusations of seeking to compete with the universities that formed part of the membership of each local network) and for adult learners (though from the outset OCNs have encompassed some achievements of school pupils), there is nothing in the specifications of the credit framework itself that is limiting by level or by age. Thus the idea of a national credit framework as a unified framework took root and developed within OCNs throughout the 1990s. By 2001, NOCN had grown to be the second largest awarding body for adult learners in the UK (NOCN, 2002) and over half a million adult learners were achieving credits every year through local networks.

The impetus for reform

Despite the continuing growth of OCNs, by the beginning of the twenty-first century it seemed that demands for the establishment of a national credit framework in England were running out of steam. However, at the same time a number of other factors were combining to create the conditions for the 'breakthrough' of credit embodied in *21st Century Skills*. Among these we may identify the following as being of key importance:

- the perceived 'failure' of the NQF to be responsive to the needs of individuals and employers (DfES, 2002b);
- in response to these needs, the continuing development of significant numbers of externally-accredited certificates outside the NQF (LSC, 2005);
- the development of credit-based initiatives in each of the other countries of the UK - i.e. the Scottish Credit and Qualifications Framework (SCQF), the Northern Ireland Credit Accumulation and Transfer Scheme (NICATS) and the Credit and Qualifications Framework for Wales (CQFW);
- the appointment of new ministers, senior civil servants and heads of key agencies with an agenda for reform;
- the positive intervention of the Cabinet Office in the debate about the potential benefits of a credit system. (Cabinet Office, 2002, 2003).

Notwithstanding all these factors, there is little doubt that the necessary positive climate for qualifications reform was created by the A Level debacle of 2002 and the high profile resignations of awarding body and regulatory authority chief executives, and subsequently a minister, in its wake. Thus, although the Tomlinson reforms are an obvious direct result of these events, there is a strong case to be made that the impetus for more general reform of the qualifications system emanates from the perceived failure of these most prized products of the existing NQF.

The ownership of a credit system

What is significant about the concept of 'credit' throughout this period is that it slowly became detached from its particular meaning within the work of OCNs and acquired a more general applicability to the recognition of achievement across all parts of the post-school sector. Lest this seems to be an accidental process we should acknowledge the fact that OCNs were among the first to recognise this potential for 'their' credit systems. Indeed, we may trace a number of partnerships, collaborations and alliances established between NOCN and other awarding bodies over the past decade that consciously sought to build on this potential for credit to form the technical basis for mutually recognising achievements beyond the boundaries of OCNs.

Thus, in order to fulfil this potential role, it has been necessary to strip away from the concept of credit all those features that lead to a particular approach to curriculum design and delivery or to the needs of a particular subject, sector or group of learners. In its journey of gradual detachment as an integral part of the OCN system to a potential part of a wider system for recognising achievement, the concept of credit can be seen to have crystallised into a technical device, devoid of any particular content, value or ideological baggage. It is this quality that makes the concept of credit so useful in developing a genuine currency of learner achievement that is potentially transferable across the post-school sector.

The key features of credit systems

Before considering the relevance of credit systems to the reform of qualifications for 14–19 year-olds, their key characteristics, developed both through the work of OCNs and through higher education institutions across England, Wales and Northern Ireland, are identified:

- the use of a standard unit template within which all achievements are represented;
- the determination of credit value as a standard measure of learner achievement;

- the award of credit for the successful achievement of units;
- the development of rules of combination based on credit achievement as the basis for qualifications design.

These four characteristics, each of which is considered briefly below, is an important feature of the concept of a credit framework as a unifying mechanism in the post-school sector.

A standard unit template

Over a decade ago, all OCNs adopted a standard specification for the units developed in all Networks. This specification was based on the proposals of the Further Education Unit in *A Basis for Credit* (FEU, 1992) and has subsequently been adopted as the basis for both the CQFW and NICATS, and for all HE members of the England, Wales and Northern Ireland credit consortia (EWNI). It is also one of the key technical specifications of the FfA. The unit specification identifies five features:

- title;
- learning outcomes;
- assessment criteria;
- level;
- credit value.

Organisations that have adopted this specification have developed many thousands of units over the past decade, in all subject and vocational areas, at all levels of achievement, and for all types of learning and assessment. The unit specification has proved to be a ubiquitous, simple and accessible device that contains the minimum amount of information necessary to establish stable levels and credit values for units, together with the flexibility in assessment methods necessary to meet the needs of a wide range of learners, providers and awarding bodies.

Credit value

Each unit leading to the award of credit is given a credit value. This is defined simply as '*the number of credits available to a learner for the successful completion of a unit*'. In turn 'credit' is defined as '*an award made to a learner for the successful completion of a unit*'. Within UK credit systems the basis for calculating credit values has been to identify the notional learning time taken by a learner to achieve the learning outcomes of a unit. Initially this calculation was based on the principle that the outcomes achievable in a notional 30 hours of learning would have a credit value of one. In recent years, this has changed to 10 hours, in order to bring credit systems at lower levels more into line with the 10-hour 'credit tariff' that operates in HE. The FfA has adopted this 10-hour tariff.

The definition of credit value can appear a clumsy device, attempting as it does to join together the concepts of process (learning time) and outcome (learner achievement) in a single specification. Nevertheless, this definition has proved to be far more elegant and robust in practice than it appears. The key is the concept of 'notionality' embedded in the definition. Credit practitioners have come to appreciate the literal value of this aspect of the definition – the joining together of the concepts of process and outcome in a single specification needs to be mediated through a sophisticated and intelligent process if it is to be applied usefully.

The determination of the credit value of a unit therefore creates a 'universal joint' that allows the deployment of a shared value (time) to a given set of information (the learning outcomes and assessment criteria of a unit) in a way that 'frees' learners, providers and assessors from any particular process constraints in valuing learner achievement. As OCNs demonstrate conclusively, credit values can be determined for any assessable and coherent set of learning outcomes without constraining the process through which these outcomes are learned and assessed. This particular method of measuring the value of learning outcomes is the basis for the potential of credit systems to provide a universal measure of achievement.

The award of credit

As credit systems have developed from grassroots practice with adult learners, they have established processes designed to meet specific needs. One of these processes is the frequent recognition of learner achievement through the award of credit. This simple principle – that credit is an award made to a learner – has been nurtured and sustained within OCNs over two decades, as alternative concepts of 'credit' (e.g. as a tool for curriculum management, as an element of a funding mechanism) have been proposed and abandoned. It is this definition that is now being taken forward into the FfA.

The definition of credit as an award means that it can become a genuine currency of learner achievement. In fact, credit displays much more obviously the classic characteristics of a currency – stability, ubiquity, liquidity and convertibility – than does a qualification. These characteristics of credit as a currency of achievement enable it to be used far more flexibly in recognising learner achievement than traditional qualifications. The recent history of OCNs illustrates just how much this potential flexibility has been deployed to meet the goals of widening participation and responsiveness to individual learner needs (Moseley *et al.*, 2004).

Rules of combination

Although the award of credit confers recognition of learner achievement on an individual learner, the award of credit on its own is not capable of creating 'exchange value' for particular combinations of achievement. (i.e. its convertibility as a currency). In order to ensure that the 'price' of a particular progression or employment opportunity is met by a learner, credits need to be organised into particular useful combinations that meet the requirements of the gatekeepers of these opportunities. The mechanisms through which credit achievements are organised to create these exchange values are 'rules of combination'.

The first systematic and structured approach to the development of rules of combination within a credit system was established in the early 1990s within the Access to Higher Education Recognition Scheme. Access to HE Certificates, therefore, offer us the first examples of the use of rules of combination that structured patterns of credit achievement into qualifications to meet the needs of learners seeking entry to HE. In 2005 the Access Recognition Scheme still offers the most developed examples of such rules in the UK (QAA, 2004).

The development of rules of combination enabled credit systems to demonstrate their capacity to address the needs not only of marginalised adult learners on short courses, but those on substantial programmes underwritten by a national quality assurance agency (now QAA) for progression to Higher Education. It also demonstrated that, in certain circumstances, the flexibility of the credit system could be tempered to meet particular requirements for progression through the application of rules of combination. Indeed, as credit is simply a currency of achievement rather than a 'good' with intrinsic value, it is capable of subjection to the most restrictive limitations through draconian rules of combination without compromise to its value in recognising achievement. It is this potential of credit-based rules of achievement to meet the needs of any type of progression conditions that creates its usefulness as a comprehensive device within the FfA.

The relevance of credit to the 14–19 reforms

As we noted earlier, there was a distinct difference in the use of language between the work of the Tomlinson Group and those responsible for the development of proposals for a new framework of credit-based qualifications targeted primarily at adult learners. Notwithstanding these distinctions, both the Tomlinson reform process and the development of credit systems represent unifying concepts to be deployed in the process of qualifications reform. This shared commitment to a unified solution to the qualifications reform agenda provides an important tie between the different traditions.

In summary, because the concept of credit and the related technical specifications that underpin the award of credit to learners are 'value free', they could be applied to the Diploma system proposed by Tomlinson without deflecting the purpose of the reforms in relation to the particular needs of 14–19 learners. Although the 14–19 White Paper has postponed the opportunity to demonstrate the potential of this application comprehensively across the curriculum, we attempt to show in the following section of this paper how the specifications of a credit system can be applied to the development of the new specialised diplomas.

Our contention here is that, while it will be both feasible and desirable to specify the design of new 14–19 Diplomas within a credit system, this is a potentially radical departure from what has traditionally been the process of development for key public qualifications. The 'credit tradition' originates not just within an adult learning context, but within an explicitly local context. The publication of *A Basis for Credit?* (FEU, 1992) marks the point at which the 'localness' of the credit tradition began its transformation into a genuinely national system. The publication of *21st Century Skills* recognised credit as an acceptable feature of all future vocational qualifications. It remains to be seen, however, whether the triple burdens of localness, 'adultness' and vocationalism can be overcome in developing the specifications of the new diplomas within the FfA.

The rationale for reform

In its work on supporting and defending the interests of adult learners over many years, NIACE has argued consistently that the needs of adult learners are different from those of younger learners. In particular, it has sought to make a distinction between younger people in full-time education or training who define themselves as 'students' and older learners in part-time learning who define themselves as 'workers', 'parents', 'carers' etc. and for whom the experience of learning is not the defining activity of their lives.

As credit systems have emerged in the UK in recent years, they have been explicitly linked to the needs of adult learners. Indeed, the various white papers and remit letters that have created the separate briefs to take forward the development of 'specialised Diplomas' and 'a credit framework' cement these differences. Policy responsibilities in this area are still divided into '14–19' and 'adult' (actually 'adult skills') remits. The current remit to LSC and QCA to take forward the development of the FfA refers specifically to its importance in supporting the Government's strategy on 'adult skills'.

From the perspectives of both government and those seeking to take forward the interests of adult learners, therefore, the principle of 'different needs' is deeply embedded. In such a context, the argument that it is possible to develop a new generation of qualifications that meet the needs of 14–19 learners, within the design features of credit-based qualifications derived explicitly from the needs of adult learners, is hard to make. Such a proposition turns on its head the traditional direction of qualifications development, where for many years qualifications have been designed to meet the needs of younger learners and then been extended to meet the needs of adults.

It now seems that we have an opportunity to reverse this particular process. The current remit for reform of 'vocational and adult' qualifications is based on an acceptance that existing qualifications are too inflexible to meet the needs of many adults, and are too narrowly focused to provide a basis for continuing employability in the twenty-first century labour market. We suggest here that, although the rationale for reform of qualifications for 14–19 year olds has a different basis, the design features of the FfA can be used to underpin the development of new Diplomas based on the principles set out in the Tomlinson Final Report. Thus, though the context for 14–19 reform within the FfA is much narrower than that proposed by Tomlinson, an opportunity now presents itself to establish a 'Diploma model' within the FfA that can illustrate the potential for bringing together the two distinct unifying traditions of English post-14 education within a single reform process. We suggest that this opportunity, though compromised by the timidity of the 14–19 White Paper, needs to be seized.

New diplomas and the

Framework for Achievement

Despite the disappointments of the 14–19 White Paper there still exists the possibility of demonstrating in the immediate future that the two unified reform traditions identified in this paper can be brought together in the development of new specialised diplomas within the FfA. In particular, the remit for their development creates the opportunity to establish the following 'unifying' design features which can guide not only the development of these specialised diplomas, but can also form the basis for the eventual entry of general education, including GCSEs and A Levels:

- the use of a standard unit specification as the building block for all diplomas;
- the development of assessment arrangements around these units that reflect the principles of a more devolved and less burdensome assessment regime set out in the Tomlinson proposals;
- the use of the principles of credit accumulation and transfer to establish the principle of 'interlocking' diplomas both across levels and across subjects/sectors;
- the development of flexible rules of combination, based on the achievement of credits, to establish the coherence of individual diplomas;
- the use of the principle of exemption to create opportunities for other awards to 'count' towards the achievement of a diploma.

All the above features will be present in all qualifications established within the FfA. Our contention here is that each of these features can be represented within the design of new diplomas in such a way as to meet the particular needs of 14–19 learners in full-time education or training. Thus a set of design features developed to meet the particular needs of adult learners could also be used to support the design of a set of qualifications for younger learners. Below, we take each of the above design features in turn and suggest ways in which they could be used to design new specialised diplomas that conform to the key design principles set out in the Tomlinson Final Report.

A standard unit format

One of the proposed features of the FfA that has received almost universal support is that all qualifications would be built from units based on a standard set of specifications. All units within the FfA will be designed within this format and will not include any additional information. Evidence from other functioning credit systems demonstrates that this simple format is applicable to all curriculum areas, subjects and sectors, and to all types of assessment arrangements. It could, therefore, be used to represent all elements of new specialised diplomas, including 'academic' and 'vocational' learning, classroom-based, work-based and project-based assessments, as well as functional literacy, numeracy and ICT skills and additional activity-based personal learning.

The unit specification for the FfA is designed to present to users the minimum information necessary to describe learner achievement. In itself the unit does not provide sufficient information to enable a valid and reliable assessment of learner achievement to be made, but provides a consistent basis for making this judgement. The additional information required relates to the particular assessment arrangements and instruments to be applied to the unit, and the FfA itself makes no assumptions about what these arrangements should be. The unit format, therefore, provides the basic design feature within which the content of all diplomas can be presented, and around which the particular arrangements for assessment of each component of the diploma can be constructed.

Reducing the burden of assessment

One of the aims of the Tomlinson proposals was to establish a less burdensome and more devolved assessment regime for new diplomas than that which has developed in recent years in GCSEs, A/AS Levels and AVCEs. The unit format for the FfA can support this aim, while at the same time addressing the issue of coherence in the learning programmes leading to the award of credits within the diploma. The relationship between assessment arrangements and the unit specification also illustrates how the design features of the FfA can be exploited to meet the different needs of different groups of learners.

In the design of qualifications targeted at adult learners within the FfA, one of the requirements is that each individual unit should be capable of separate assessment leading to the award of credit. This is a design feature aimed at creating more responsive and flexible ways of recognising learner achievements – one of the key aims behind the qualifications reform programme driven by the Skills Strategy. The rationale for qualifications reform driven by the 14–19 White Paper is different. Here entitlement, coherence and preparation for working life are key aims, rather than flexibility and responsiveness. The design of the FfA is also capable of realising these.

In particular, the separation of assessment methods from assessment criteria within the unit specification would enable the development of assessment arrangements within the Diploma that relate to a cluster of units rather than to each individual unit. Thus a group of units could be organised into a 'component' of the diploma, and assessment arrangements could be established for the whole component. These assessment arrangements might include the development of additional achievement criteria over and above the assessment criteria of individual units, which would permit grading of each component through the process of assessment.

An element of flexibility would be lost, in that learners could not achieve individual credits at unit level, but would only be awarded credits for completion of the whole component. This needs to be balanced against the gains in reducing the burden of assessment and the use of integrated assessment around components to support the coherence of the learner's experience of programmes leading to a diploma. This 'component-based' assessment need not be applied to all aspects of the diploma. It may be appropriate to apply it to the 'main learning' elements of the diploma, while the 'functional skills' elements might be assessed at the level of the individual unit.

In summary, the separation of assessment methodology from assessment criteria within the FfA unit template will permit the new diplomas to draw on the same units used to support other qualifications within the FfA, without necessarily adopting the same assessment methods and instruments used for these qualifications. There is no technical impediment within the FfA specifications that will prevent the development of an assessment regime for diplomas along the lines suggested in the Tomlinson Report.

Credit accumulation and transfer

One of the key features of the proposals of the 14–19 Working Group was that the new diplomas should 'interlock' across different levels. By this the group meant that some achievements gained on a Level One ('Foundation') diploma might also contribute to the requirements of a diploma at Level Two, and so on. In addition to this 'interlocking' across levels, the Working Group also envisaged that individual 'main learning' components might contribute to more than one specialised diploma, while of course functional literacy, numeracy and ICT skills would be present in all diplomas.

This series of inter-relationships between different elements of the diplomas can be simply and effectively supported through the system of credit accumulation and transfer that will underpin all qualifications within the FfA. It would be a straightforward task to design rules of combination for diplomas that permitted a given number of credits at a previous level of achievement to be transferred towards a diploma at the next level of the Framework. Similarly, transferring credits from individual components across diploma boundaries is a standard design feature of all qualifications within the FfA.

The representation of these design features through the FfA's credit system could bring additional flexibility into the design of diplomas, if these were seen as desirable features by those responsible. For example:

- The rules of combination could be used to set permitted limits on the ability to transfer credits from lower levels of achievement towards a diploma at a higher level, within each separate component.
- The credit system of the FfA would enable the concept of 'equivalent value' to be established between different diplomas. Rules of combination for a diploma might be expressed in terms of the requirements to achieve a specified number of credits at a particular level in a broad subject or sector, without necessarily specifying precisely the curriculum requirements of that subject or sector.
- The principle of 'interlocking' awards through credit accumulation and transfer could be used to offer the opportunity to complete specialist qualifications as part of an overall diploma. Thus, individual credits might be accumulated towards small 'interim' targets as well as towards the overall diploma.
- Some flexibility in the combination of main learning components might be introduced by setting a range of credit accumulation targets for each component, allowing components of different sizes to contribute to a diploma, while still specifying a proportion of such components that would constitute its 'main learning' programme.

It should be emphasised that these are possible, rather than necessary, design features of new diplomas that could be supported by the FfA's credit system. The system of credit accumulation and transfer will permit the maximum flexibility in the design of diplomas that is consistent with the rationale and purpose behind each individual diploma. What the credit system offers is a simple and accessible structure, presented in a straightforward language that can help all users to understand the structure of diplomas, while permitting maximum flexibility for learners in achieving them.

Rules of combination

Within the FfA, all qualifications will be designed around a set of rules of combination that set out the requirements for credit achievement in particular units at particular levels. As we have noted above, the possibility exists for units leading to the award of credit to be clustered into components for the purposes of assessment within individual diplomas. This clustering is one mechanism through which the design principle of 'coherence' in individual programmes of learning could be built into each diploma.

The rules of combination for diplomas offer another mechanism through which this principle of coherence can be manifested. The standard format for such rules within the FfA offers the designers of diplomas all the opportunities they will need to ensure that the particular combinations of credits required to achieve a diploma establish an appropriate balance between individual learner choice and the coherence of programmes leading to that diploma. There is no reason why, within an overall set of design principles, the rules of combination for each individual diploma might not be different at different levels of the Framework.

The process of accreditation of qualifications within the FfA will explicitly separate out the approval of rules of combination from the development of the units that form the basic building blocks for all qualifications. This means that, over time, the rules of combination for individual diplomas could be changed without re-designing the overall qualification. So, for example, additional options might be added to some routes to a diploma; the range of units available within one component might be expanded to reflect innovation in a particular sector; the balance between 'main learning' and other components of individual diplomas might be adjusted over time. The specifications of the FfA therefore permit a degree of 'future-proofing' of qualifications as a standard feature of their development. Again, such a design feature reflects the intentions of the 14–19 Working Group.

The principle of exemption

One of the design principles of the FfA is that learners should not have to repeat learning where their existing achievements are still relevant for the qualifications they wish to achieve within the Framework. As the above examples illustrate, where these achievements are recorded through the award of credit, this principle is enacted through the facility to transfer credits between qualifications and awarding bodies. However, many learners may wish to take advantage of this principle on the basis of qualifications achieved outside the FfA. We anticipate that learners will wish to 'count' previous achievements certificated outside the FfA towards qualifications within it, for many years to come. This facility will be established through the principle of exemption.

In essence, exemption will create the opportunity for learners to 'count' certificated achievements outside the FfA towards a qualification within it. This will be done through a process that confirms that this alternative achievement entitles the learner to be exempted from the requirement to achieve a certain number of credits within the rules of combination for that qualification. In other words, a qualification within the FfA may be achieved through the accumulation of credits or through a combination of credit accumulation and exemption. In this case, 'exemption' refers to 'exemption from the necessity to achieve credit(s)' not 'exemption from meeting the requirements of the qualification'.

The exemption facility within the FfA could, therefore, be used to provide a further flexibility within the rules of combination for diplomas. In particular, this design feature could be employed to enable exemption to be given from whole components of a diploma on the basis of the achievement of an agreed equivalent. These equivalents might be, for example, a GCSE or an A Level. Of course, many other qualifications might also be identified for exemption, and each of these possibilities could be built in to the design features of each diploma. Again, the rules of combination within the FfA include details of all such exemptions.

This is a potentially critical design feature of diplomas that will permit the 'interlocking' of achievements with GCSEs and A Levels (for as long as these qualifications continue to exist) within a coherent set of design features consistent with all other qualifications within the FfA. Thus, rather than conceiving diplomas as a 'hybrid' form of certification that straddles the regulatory boundaries between the FfA and GCSEs/A Levels, the principle of exemption enables diplomas to be specified wholly within the FfA, while permitting other achievements outside the FfA to count towards them. We may envisage a future in which some learners achieve a diploma solely through the accumulation of credits, while others achieve the same diploma through a combination of credit achievement and exemption based on GCSEs, A Levels or other identified qualifications. In both of these instances, a single set of rules of combination will apply, which set out the opportunities for these different routes to achievement.

Conclusion: not 'if' but 'when'

Bringing together the two unifying traditions promises both coherence and flexibility in the 14–19 curriculum. The Tomlinson baccalaureate/diploma proposals offer a framework for realising the curriculum purposes of 14–19 learning. The FfA provides tools for flexibility and, as we have argued here, for a more gradual approach to qualifications reform.

Developing specialised diplomas using these FfA design principles could produce a situation in which GCSEs and A Levels look increasingly isolated and out of synch with wider innovations within the system. Their reform (possibly from 2008 onwards) would become irresistible as the benefits of a holistic and flexible approach to 14+ education and training became obvious. Ken Boston (2005) recently pointed to the logic of gradual but overwhelming reform when he commented,

> *In ten years time, we must jointly have built a public consensus, so that the question will no longer be, as it was early this year 'Why would you incorporate A levels and GCSEs within a diploma structure?' The question will be 'Why would you not?'*

Of course, in the future a government could decide that it wished to phase out GCSEs and A Levels altogether and to replace them with a single system of diplomas. The previous examples of agreed equivalences between these qualifications and identified components of diplomas, established through arrangements for exemption within rules of combination, would provide a secure and accessible model of transition that could be implemented in a relatively short period of time without any disruption to the design features of the FfA. But that is another story...

References

Adams, R. (2003) 'The Welsh Baccalaureate Qualification' in Philips, G. and Pound, T. (eds) *The Baccalaureate: A Model for Curriculum Reform* London: Kogan Page.

Association for Colleges (AfC), Girls' School Association (GSA), The Headmasters' Conference (HMC), Secondary Heads' Association (SHA), Sixth Form Colleges' Association (APVIC), The Society for Headmasters and Headmistresses in Independent Schools (SHMHMIS) (1994) *Post-Compulsory Education and Training: A Joint Statement* London: AfC.

AoC, ATL, GSA, HMC, NAHT, NASUWT, NATFHE, NUT, PAT, SHA, SHMIS (1997) *Key Principles for Curriculum and Qualifications Reform from 14+* London: Post-16 Education Centre, Institute of Education, University of London.

Blackstone, T. (1998) *Qualifying for Success: The Response to the Qualifications and Curriculum Authority Advice* London: DfES.

Boston, K. (2005) *Putting the Learner First: Creating a 14–90 Future from the 14–19 White Paper* speech to the QCA Association of Learning Providers Conference, 11 May 2005.

Burgess, M. (1993) 'Linking BTEC and A/AS Levels' in Richardson, W., Woolhouse, J., & Finegold, D. (eds) *The Reform of Post-16 Education and Training in England and Wales* Harlow: Longman.

Butler, P. (2003) 'The college diploma: a case-study' in Philips, G. and Pound, T. (eds) *The Baccalaureate: A model for Curriculum Reform* London: Kogan Page.

Cabinet Office Strategy Unit (2002, 2003) *In Demand: Adult Skills in the 21st Century* London: Cabinet Office.

Crombie-White, R., Pring, R. and Brockington, D. (1995) *14–19 Education and Training: Implementing a Unified System of Learning* London: Royal Society of Arts.

CNAA (1989) *Credits for Change: The CNAA Credit Accumulation and Transfer Scheme* London: CNAA.

Dearing, Sir R. (1996) *Review of Qualifications for 16–19 Year Olds* London: SCAA.

Department for Education and Science (DES) (1988) *Advancing A Levels: Report of the Committee chaired by Professor Higginson* London: HMSO.

Department for Education (DfE)/Employment Department (ED)/Welsh Office (WO) (1991) *Education and Training for the 21st Century* London: HMSO.

Department for Education and Employment (DfEE) (1997) *Qualifying for Success: A Consultation Paper on the Future of Post-16 Qualifications* London: DfEE.

DfES (2002a) *14–19: Extending Opportunities, Raising Standards* London: The Stationery Office.

DfES (2002b) *Qualifications and Curriculum Authority Quinquennial Review* London: DfES.

DfES (2003) *14–19: Opportunity and Excellence: Government Response to the 14–19 Green Paper* London: DfES.

DfES (2005a) *14–19 Education and Skills* London: DfES.

DfES (2005b) *Letter from Phil Hope, Parliamentary Under Secretary for Skills, to Ken Boston, Chief Executive of QCA* July 18th 2005.

DfES, DTI, HM Treasury and DWP (2003) *21st Century Skills: Realising our Potential* Norwich: Stationary Office.

Evans, K., Hodkinson, P., Keep, E., Maguire, M., Raffe, D., Rainbird, H., Senker, P. and Unwin, L. (1997) *Working to Learn. Issues in People*

Management No 18 London: Institute of Personnel and Development.

Finegold, D., Keep, E., Miliband, D., Raffe, D., Spours, K. and Young, M. (1990) *A British Baccalaureate: Overcoming Divisions Between Education and Training* London: IPPR.

Further Education Development Agency (FEDA) and Institute of Education (IoE) (1999) *An Overarching Certificate at Advanced Level: Research for ACCAC, CCEA and QCA* London: FEDA.

Further Education Unit (FEU) (1992) *A Basis for Credit?* London: FEU.

FEU (1993) *Discussing Credit: A Collection of Occasional Papers Relating to the FEU Proposal for a Post-16 Credit Accumulation and Transfer Framework* London: FEU.

Higham, J. and Yeomans, D. (2005) Policy Memory and Policy Amnesia in 14–19 Education: Learning from the Past? Discussion Paper 5 for a seminar on Policy Learning in 14–19 Education, Nuffield Foundation 15 March 2005 (http://www.nuffield14–19review.org.uk).

Hodgson, A. and Spours, K. (eds) (1997) *Dearing and Beyond: 14–19 Qualifications, Frameworks and Systems* London: Kogan Page.

Hodgson, A. and Spours, K. (1999) *New Labour's Educational Agenda: Issues and Policies for Education and Training from 14+* London: Kogan Page.

Hodgson, A. and Spours, K. (2000) *An Historical and Analytical Examination of the Concept of a Graduation Certificate* London: Lifelong Learning Group, Institute of Education, University of London.

Hodgson, A. and Spours, K. (2003) *Beyond A Levels: Curriculum 2000 and the Reform of 14–19 Qualifications* London: Kogan Page.

Howieson, C., Raffe, D., Spours, K and Young, M. (1997) 'Unifying academic and vocational learning: the state of the debate in England and Scotland' *Journal of Education and Work*, 10(1): 5–35.

Jenkins, C. and David, J. (1996) *The Welsh Baccalaureate* Cardiff: Institute of Welsh Affairs.

Joint Associations' Curriculum Group (JACG) (1997) *The Next Step Towards a New Curriculum Framework Post-16* Wigan: JACG.

Labour Party (1996) *Aiming Higher: Labour's Proposals for the Reform of the 14–19 Curriculum* London: Labour Party.

Labour Party (1997) *Labour Party General Election Manifesto 1997: Because Britain Deserves Better* London: Labour Party.

Lasonen, J. (1998) *Reforming Upper Secondary Education in Europe: Surveys of Strategies for Post-16 Education to Improve the Parity of Esteem for Initial Vocational Education in Eight European Educational Systems* Finland: University of Jyvaskyla Press.

Learning and Skills Council (2005) *Statistical First Release: Learner Outcomes in England 2003–04* Coventry: LSC.

Moseley, R. *et al.* (2005) *The Impact of Unit-based Credit Frameworks (Report to LSC)* Warwick: University of Warwick.

National Association of Headteachers (NAHT) (1995) *Proposals on 14–19 Education* Haywards Heath: NAHT.

National Commission on Education (NCE) (1995*) Learning to Succeed: The Way Ahead Report of Paul Hamlyn Foundation National Commission on Education* London: NCE.

National Institute for Adult Continuing Education (1991) *The National Open College Network: A position statement* London: UDACE.

National Open College Network (2002) *Annual Review 2002* Derby: NOCN.

National Union of Teachers (NUT) (1995) *14–19 Strategy for the Future: The Road to Equality* London: NUT.

Quality Assurance Agency for Higher Education (2004) *Access to Higher Education Development Project* Gloucester: QAA.

QCA/ACCAC/CCEA (1998) *An Overarching Certificate at Advanced Level: Research Specification* London: QCA.

QCA (2004) *New Thinking for Reform: A Framework for Achievement* London: QCA.

QCA and the Learning and Skills Council (LSC) (2004) *Principles for a Credit Framework for England* London: QCA.

Richardson, W., Spours, K., Woolhouse, J. and Young, M. (1995) *Learning for the Future Interim Report* Post-16 London and Warwick: Education Centre, Institute of Education, University of London and Centre for Education and Industry, University of Warwick.

Royal Society (1991) *Beyond GCSE: A Report by a Working Group of the Royal Society's Education Committee* London: The Royal Society.

Social Exclusion Unit (SEU) (1999) *Bridging the Gap: New Opportunities for 16–18 Year Olds Not in Education, Employment or Training* London: SEU.

Stewart, J. (2003) 'George Abbott School and the Surrey Graduation Certificate' in Philips, G. and Pound, T. (eds) *The Baccalaureate: A Model for Curriculum Reform* London: Kogan Page.

Unit for the Development of Adult Continuing Education (UDACE) (1991) *Open College Networks: Current developments and practice* Leicester: NIACE.

Working Group on 14–19 Reform (2003) *Principles for Reform of 14–19 Learning Programmes and Qualifications: Progress Report* London: DfES.

Working Group on 14–19 Reform (2004a) *14–19 Curriculum and Qualifications Reform: Interim Report* London: DfES.

Working Group on 14–19 Reform (2004b) *14–19 Curriculum and Qualifications Reform: Final Report* London: DfES.

Young, M. and Spours, K. (1996) *Post-Compulsory Curriculum and Qualifications: Options for Change* London and Warwick: Institute of Education, University of London and Centre for Education and Industry, University of Warwick.